METAMORPHOSES

METAMORPHOSES

A Play

Based on David R. Slavitt's translation
of *The Metamorphoses of Ovid*

———————

MARY ZIMMERMAN

NORTHWESTERN UNIVERSITY PRESS
EVANSTON, ILLINOIS

Northwestern University Press
Evanston, Illinois 60208-4210

Printed in the United States of America

10 9 8 7 6 5 4 3 2 1

ISBN 0-8101-1978-1 (cloth)
ISBN 0-8101-1980-3 (paper)

Based on David R. Slavitt's translation of *The Metamorphoses of Ovid*, published by The Johns Hopkins University Press in 1994.

The Rilke portion of "Orpheus and Eurydice" is from Stephen Mitchell's translation of Rainer Maria Rilke's "Orpheus. Eurydice. Hermes," in *The Selected Poetry of Rainer Maria Rilke*, published by Random House in 1987. Copyright © 1980, 1981, and 1982 by Stephen Mitchell.

"Kingfisher's Song" is based on David A. Campbell's translation of an anonymous lyric in *Greek Lyric Poetry: A Selection of Early Greek Lyric, Elegiac and Iambic Poetry*, published by St. Martin's Press in 1967.

The author wishes to acknowledge the influence of the work of C. G. Jung, Sigmund Freud, James Hillman, and Joseph Campbell in the "Phaeton" and "Eros and Psyche" scenes.

Library of Congress Cataloging-in-Publication data are available from the Library of Congress.

The paper used in this publication meets the minimum requirements of the American National Standard for Information Sciences—Permanence of Paper for Printed Library Materials, ANSI Z39.48-1984.

To the Cast and Designers and Anjali

CONTENTS

PHOTOGRAPHS

Gallery of photographs follows page 86.

PRODUCTION HISTORY

An early version of *Metamorphoses*, entitled *Six Myths*, was produced at the Theatre and Interpretation Center of Northwestern University, Evanston, Illinois, in May 1996.

The world premiere of *Metamorphoses* was produced by Lookingglass Theatre Company, Chicago, and opened on October 25, 1998, at the Ivanhoe Theatre.

Myrrha and others . . . . Anjali Bhimani

Vertumnus and others . . . . Lawrence E. DiStasi

Nursemaid and others . . . . Marilyn Dodds Frank

Aphrodite and others . . . . Anne Dudek

Midas and others . . . . Raymond Fox

Phaeton and others . . . . Doug Hara

Erysichthon and others . . . . Chris Kipiniak

Alcyone and others . . . . Louise Lamson

Orpheus and others . . . . Erik Lochtefeld

Eurydice and others . . . . Heidi Stillman

The Second Stage Theatre production opened in New York City on October 9, 2001.

Myrrha and others . . . . Anjali Bhimani

Vertumnus and others . . . . Kyle Hall

Nursemaid and others . . . . Lisa Tejero

Aphrodite and others . . . . Felicity Jones

Midas and others . . . . Raymond Fox

Phaeton and others . . . . Doug Hara

Erysichthon and others . . . . Chris Kipiniak

Alcyone and others . . . . Louise Lamson
Orpheus and others . . . . Erik Lochtefeld
Eurydice and others . . . . Heidi Stillman

The Broadway production opened at Circle in the Square, New York, on March 4, 2002, and had the same cast as Second Stage, with the exception of Mariann Mayberry for Eurydice and others. It was produced by Roy Gabay, Robyn Goodman, Allan S. Gordon, Élan V. McAllister, D. Harris/M. Swinsky, Ruth Hendel, Sharon Karmazin, R. L. Wreghitt/ J. Bergère.

Metamorphoses has also been produced at the Berkeley Repertory Theatre, the Seattle Repertory Theatre, and the Mark Taper Forum in Los Angeles.

For all professional productions, Daniel Ostling designed the set, T. J. Gerckens designed the lights, Mara Blumenfeld designed the costumes, Andre Pluess and Ben Sussman did the sound design, and the music was composed by Willy Schwarz. Anjali Bidani was Production Stage Manager for all productions, except for Broadway, where she stage-managed with the addition of Debra A. Acquavella as Production Stage Manager.

METAMORPHOSES

A NOTE ON THE STAGING

The stage is entirely occupied by a square or rectangular pool of water, of varying depth, bordered on all four sides by a wooden deck approximately three feet wide. Hanging above the pool is a large crystal chandelier. Upstage, there is a large painting of the sky, above which gods and goddesses might appear. Also upstage is a tall double door, with steps leading to it from the deck. Ideally, there should be six entrances to the playing area: one on each of the deck's four corners, one through the doors, and one between the doors and sky. Additionally, there is a platform for the actors behind the sky, with its own entrance and exit. The set has sat well in both thrust and proscenium theaters, but it is essential that the audience look down at the playing space in such a way that the entire surface of the water is visible.

All scenes take place in and around the pool, with shifts between stories, scenes, and settings indicated by nothing more than a shift in light or merely a shift in the actors' orientation or perhaps a music cue. Although there is a great deal of narration in the play, it should not be taken as a substitute for action or a superfluous description of action: The staging should rarely be a literal embodiment of the text; rather, it should provide images that amplify the text, lend it poetic resonance, or, even, sometimes contradict it.

CHARACTERS

Woman by the Water
Scientist
Zeus
Three Laundresses
Midas and His Daughter
Silenus
Bacchus
Ceyx, a King
Alcyone, His Wife
Hermes
Aphrodite
Erysichthon and His Mother
Orpheus
Eurydice, His Bride
Vertumnus, God of Springtime
Pomona, a Wood Nymph
Cinyras, a King
Myrrha, His Daughter
Nursemaid, Her Nurse
Phaeton
Therapist
Eros
Psyche
Q and A
Baucis, a Poor Woman
Philemon, Her Husband

In addition, there are several important narrators, servants, sailors, other gods and goddesses, denizens of the Underworld, spirits, and so forth.

[*A* WOMAN *is kneeling by the side of the pool, looking at her own re-flection. She looks up and addresses the audience.*]

WOMAN:
Bodies, I have in mind, and how they can change to assume
new shapes—I ask the help of the gods, who know the trick:
change me, and let me glimpse the secret and speak,
better than I know how, of the world's birthing,
and the creation of all things, from the first to the very latest.

[*The* SCIENTIST *enters, wearing a lab coat and shaking a jar of water and sand. As she speaks she walks forward, sets the jar down, and the elements separate.*]

SCIENTIST:
Before there was water and dry land, or even heaven and earth,
nature was all the same: what we call "chaos,"
with neither sun to shed its light, nor moon to wax
and wane, nor earth hung in its atmosphere of air.
If there was land and sea, there was no discernible shoreline,
no way to walk on the one, or swim or sail in the other.
There was neither reason nor order, until at last, a god sparked,

[ZEUS appears above the sky. He lights a cigarette.]

glowed, then shone like a beam of light to define earth
and the heavens and separate water from hard ground.

WOMAN:
Once these distinctions were made and matter began to behave,
the sky displayed its array of stars in their constellations—

[The lights of the chandelier begin to glow.]

a twinkling template of order. The sea upon which they shone
quickened with fish, and the woods and meadows with game,
and the air with twittering birds. Each order of creature
settling into itself.

ZEUS:
A paradise, it would seem, except one thing was lacking: words.

WOMAN:
And so

[MIDAS enters through the doors.]

WOMAN:
man was born. He was born that he might

[MIDAS comes forward and steps into the water.]

WOMAN:
talk.

ZEUS:
Some say the god perfected the world,
creating of his divine substance the race of humans;

SCIENTIST:
others maintain that we come from the natural order of things.

[*Two* LAUNDRESSES *enter with a dreamy air, carrying a basket of laundry.*]

WOMAN:
But one way or another, people came—erect, standing tall,
with our faces set not to gaze down at the dirt beneath our feet,
but upward toward the sky in pride or, perhaps, nostalgia.

MIDAS

[ZEUS *and the* WOMAN *depart. The* SCIENTIST *takes off her lab coat and joins the* LAUNDRESSES. *The trio settles. Two of the women dip linens into the pool while the* FIRST LAUNDRESS *lounges.*]

FIRST LAUNDRESS:
What would you do with all the money in the world?

SECOND LAUNDRESS:
What a question.

FIRST LAUNDRESS:
I know what I'd do. [*Pause.*] Do you want to know what I'd do?

SECOND LAUNDRESS:
No.

FIRST LAUNDRESS:
I'd never do laundry again.

SECOND LAUNDRESS:
That's it. That's the big dream?

FIRST LAUNDRESS:
Among other things.

SECOND LAUNDRESS:
Do you want to hear a little story?

FIRST LAUNDRESS:
About rich people?

SECOND LAUNDRESS:
Yes.

FIRST LAUNDRESS:
Always!

SECOND LAUNDRESS:
There was a certain king, named Midas. Net worth: one hundred billion.

[*As* MIDAS *begins to speak, his young* DAUGHTER *comes out, bouncing a red ball.*]

MIDAS:
Now, I'm not a greedy man, but it is an accepted fact—a proven fact—that money is a good thing. A thing to be longed for, a *necessary* thing. And my god, I have a lot of it! It wasn't always this way

8

with me—the boats, the houses by the sea, the summer cottages and the winter palaces, the exotic furnishings, the soft clothes, the food and—

[*To his* DAUGHTER.]

Honey, can you stop that now? Be still now. Daddy's talking.

[*She stops, momentarily.* MIDAS *turns back to the audience.*]

Excuse me. The outrageous food and two-hundred-year-old wine. No, it wasn't always like this. I came up from poor and I worked hard all my life. Still do, mind you. My father was a minor manufacturer in [*he can't remember*] . . . somewhere . . . in . . . somewhere. But I was born with a head for business and it's always been as though everything I touched has turned to gold. Not literally, of course—wouldn't that be something? Turned a profit, I meant. And—

[*Again to his* DAUGHTER.]

Sweetheart. Daddy asked you: Be still. Take it inside.

[*She retreats but shortly reenters, jumping rope.*]

You see this pool? It cost a pretty penny, I can tell you. But all it takes is hard work. Plain and simple. And those who haven't got it in them, well, what can anyone do? They just haven't got it.

[*To his* DAUGHTER.]

Be still! You're driving me nuts already!—

[*To the audience.*]

But you know, I never forget that I do it all for my [*he can't remember*] . . . let's see, all for my . . . it's all for the, uh . . . for the, um . . . the *family*. Yes, that's what it's all for. Family is the most important thing, isn't it? One's own family, I mean—not anyone else's for god's sake. When I get home at midnight seven days a week, in the moments before sleep, I realize that . . . um . . . I realize . . . what was I—? Oh yes, that the family is what really matters.

[*A* SERVANT *enters.*]

SERVANT:
Sir—?

MIDAS:
Yes, what is it?

[SILENUS *enters, drunk, vine leaves in his hair, wearing a leopard-skin skirt and holding a wine bottle in a brown paper bag and some chips.*]

SERVANT:
This man's been making trouble in the town. We believe he is a vagrant, sir, of the worst, most drunken kind.

SILENUS:
Hello, King!

SERVANT:
What should we do?

SILENUS:
Nice place!

SERVANT:
Execute him?

MIDAS:
No need, no need. In my day, I've certainly been three sheets to the wind.

SILENUS:
Three sheets to the—? What—? What the hell are you talking about, King? I'm all rummed up!

MIDAS:
Why even last week at the feast for—

SILENUS:
Let me tell you something. You know what?

MIDAS:
No, what?

SILENUS:
Let me tell you—

MIDAS:
Yes?

SILENUS:
Let me tell you something.

MIDAS:
Yes, all right.

SILENUS:
I've been all over the world.

[*He settles into the pool, beside* MIDAS.]

MIDAS:
Oh, have you?

SILENUS:
Yes. I—I'm lost now. But I have been—all over the place.

MIDAS:
Mmm. How nice for you.

SILENUS:
You listening? Well, let me tell you there is a country beyond this one, where . . . uh . . .

MIDAS:
How very fascinating. Well, if you will excuse me—

SILENUS:
No. Listen. I strayed from the crowd, and I'm lost now, but there is a country—

MIDAS:
Asia?

SILENUS:
Further.

MIDAS:
Africa?

SILENUS:
No. Further. Over the ocean. I've been there.

MIDAS:
Oh?

SILENUS:
King, I tell ya, it's like a dream, a dream. I. Am. Telling. You. That in this place the people . . . they see each other. And in this place they live without desire of any kind and so time? There is no time—just the blue sky above and the pretty moon at night and they got the meadows under their feet with the yellow flowers and—

MIDAS:
Well, thank you, this has been most entertaining, but—

SILENUS:
And the people live forever.

MIDAS:
What?

[MIDAS'S DAUGHTER *begins to skip rope.*]

SILENUS:
They live forever. They never die.

MIDAS:
What is it, some herb they have, some . . .

SILENUS:
Oh, no. No no no.

MIDAS:
Something in the air? Something we could distill? I have shipping fleets you know to bring it—

SILENUS:
No, no. It's—

MIDAS:
Yes?

SILENUS:
Is that your daughter?

MIDAS:
What? Yes. [*To her.*] Go on, get out of here! Be still for once in your life! [*To him.*] Go on, go on.

[*She retreats for good.*]

SILENUS:
You're rich indeed.

MIDAS:
Go on. Is it an animal? Even better if it's an animal, we could breed them here. My god, the millions! Don't worry, young man, you'll get your cut—

SILENUS:
No. Nope. No.

MIDAS:
It's not an animal? What is it? What is this secret to eternal life?

SILENUS [*pointing to his own head*]:
It's here.

MIDAS:
Some formula, you have it? The formula?

SILENUS:
No, no. It's here [*pointing to* MIDAS*'s head*].

MIDAS:
What?

SILENUS:
And here [*pointing to* MIDAS*'s heart*].

MIDAS:
Oh, that. The "inner life." What uselessness. All right then. Off you go. You may sleep in the cabana.

SILENUS:
Thank you. [*He falls drunkenly, facedown in the water.*]

MIDAS:
Oh for god's sake, turn him over. Someone turn him over before he drowns.

[*The* SERVANT, *with distaste, goes into the pool and turns* SILENUS *over with his foot.*]

SECOND LAUNDRESS:
Night fell, but when the rosy-fingered dawn came back again—

BACCHUS [*entering drunkenly above, behind the sky*]:
Midas?

MIDAS:
Good lord! Who's there?

BACCHUS:
It's Bacchus. I hear you have a follower of mine.

MIDAS:
A follower?

BACCHUS:
Yes, Silenus. He wandered from our group as we passed close to town and I hear he is with you.

MIDAS:
Oh, the fellow in the cabana? Yes, take him, he's all yours.

[SILENUS *rises and exits.*]

BACCHUS [*lachrymose*]:
I'm grateful that you didn't turn him away, Midas, that you took care of him and saw that he didn't drown in his condition. And I'd like to present you with a gift.

MIDAS:
A gift?

BACCHUS:
Some ability. A minor miracle. Something to do at parties?

MIDAS:
Anything?

[SILENUS *appears above the clouds with* BACCHUS.]

BACCHUS:
Anything at all.

MIDAS:
You promise?

BACCHUS:
Yes, of course.

MIDAS:
Then grant me that everything I touch, everything I put my hand to, will turn to solid gold.

[*Long pause.*]

BACCHUS:
That's a really, really bad idea.

MIDAS:
What do you mean it's a bad idea? It's a brilliant idea!

BACCHUS:
Think about it, Midas.

MIDAS:
No, you think about it! You gave your oath. We had a deal for god's sake. Now follow through!

BACCHUS:
All right then.

[BACCHUS *and* SILENUS *exit.*]

SECOND LAUNDRESS:
And from that moment on, everything he touched turned to solid gold.

MIDAS:
Wait a minute, wait a minute, let me think where to begin . . .

[MIDAS *reaches into the water, picks up a large seashell. It is gold. He becomes giddy. He places the shell on his chair and then begins to walk around the deck. From now on, each of his steps is accompanied by the ring of little finger cymbals, perhaps played by one of the* LAUNDRESSES.]

SECOND LAUNDRESS:
He went out walking and with every step, the gravel under his feet turned to golden nuggets. Delighted, he put his hand to branches of trees and to flowers and he had gold branches and flowers. All day long he experimented, almost insane with happiness, that the whole of the world could become his personal treasure. Late at night, he stumbled back into the courtyard, laden with precious gold.

MIDAS'S DAUGHTER [*entering and running toward him*]:
Papa!

MIDAS:
NO!

[*It's too late. She jumps into his arms and turns to gold.* BACCHUS *re-enters.*]

Take it away. [*Pause.*] Bacchus, [*pause*] take it away.

BACCHUS:
I can't.

MIDAS:
Yes you can. You must. Take it away now.

BACCHUS:
I'm sorry.

MIDAS:
No, take it away, now!

BACCHUS:
There is one way, Midas.

MIDAS:
What? What is it?

BACCHUS:
Walk as far as the ends of the earth. Look for a pool of water that reflects the stars at night. Wash your hands in it and there is a chance that everything will be restored.

[MIDAS *slowly walks away, his steps accompanied by the ringing cymbals. He reaches behind the desk and picks up his* DAUGHTER's *jump-rope. It has turned to gold.*]

SECOND LAUNDRESS:
Was that too sad for you?

THIRD LAUNDRESS:
A little.

SECOND LAUNDRESS:
All right then, here's another.

ALCYONE AND CEYX

[*Music. Transition. The* SECOND LAUNDRESS *becomes the* NARRATOR *of the following story.* ALCYONE *and* CEYX *enter variously.*]

NARRATOR:
There once was a king named Ceyx who had as his queen Alcyone,
daughter of Aeolus, master of the winds. These two
adored each other and lived in a monotony of happiness.
But nothing in this world is safe.

ALCYONE:
It isn't true.

CEYX:
It is.

NARRATOR:
One day Alcyone had heard that Ceyx had ordered his ship to be
made ready for a sea voyage, to visit a far-off oracle.

ALCYONE:

How can you leave me alone? I'll pine in your absence.
Overland, it's a long and arduous trip, but I'd still prefer that
to a voyage by sea—which I fear, for my father's winds are wild and
     savage.
You think as his son-in-law you may get some special treatment. Not
     so!
Once they've escaped my father's cave, those winds are wild
and beyond anyone's control. As a girl I watched them come home
exhausted and spent, and I learned to fear them then.
Now I am petrified, surely—

NARRATOR:

she said,

ALCYONE:

          if you die my life is over
and I shall be cursed with every reluctant breath I draw.

CEYX:

My love, I hate to choose between my journey and you
but how can I live this way? Stranded on shore, afraid,
domesticated, diminished, a kind of lap dog?

ALCYONE:

Take me with you at least, and we'll meet the storms together,
which I fear much less than to be left a widow.

CEYX:

In two months' time, I'll be back.

ALCYONE:

No. I fear you won't. I know you won't.

CEYX:

In two months' time. For that short time, you can be brave
and endure the trial of waiting.

NARRATOR:

She was hardly consoled, but she saw she could not hold out any
  longer
in the face of his resolve. She allowed herself to be soothed
and consented to his going.

[*Music begins and continues through the next long sequence.* SAIL-
ORS *enter with oars.*]

There were no more details left to be checked,
no last-minute changes to make, and the men, arranged on their
  benches,
were ready to row and go. He boarded and gave the sign.
And then he turned to wave at her.
She waved at him while the ribbon of black water widened between
  the ship
and shore. She gazed at him until he was no longer distinguishable
but still she could see the ship. And she narrowed her eyes to the
  horizon
and watched it as it receded to a smaller and smaller object. And then
the whole hull was gone, and only the sails remained,
and then they, too, disappeared.
She gazed still at the empty and desolate blue
and then went to her empty bedroom to lie on the huge
and vacant bed and give herself over to weeping.

CEYX:

The vessel cleared the harbor and caught the freshening wind,

which set the rigging to singing and slapping against the spars.
I ordered the rowers to ship their oars and the sailors
to set the yards and make sail. Our ship ran before the wind.
We made satisfactory progress all that day and had reached
a point of no return, with as much blue water astern
as remained ahead.

NARRATOR:
But as the sun was sinking in the West, the water,
everywhere blue until now, began to be flecked
with the whitecapped waves sailors dislike.

[*Enter* POSEIDON *and his* HENCHMAN.]

The weather was worse with every moment
for the winds were on the loose.

[*The storm begins.* POSEIDON *and his* HENCHMAN *attack* CEYX, *the boat,
the* SAILORS.]

CEYX:
Reef the sails! Bail the water! Secure the spars!

NARRATOR:
But Poseidon and his Henchman had arrived. The rest
was one enormous green catastrophe.

[*The storm escalates. The chandelier flashes as though it were light-
ning or as if it were a lamp shorting out. The men wrestle in the pool.*]

CEYX:
He thinks in an oddly abstracted way that the waves are lions

crazed with hunters' wounds, or that the ship
is a besieged town attacked by a horde of madmen.

HENCHMAN AND CEYX:
One would think that the heavens were crazed with lust

CEYX:
to join the turbulent sea

HENCHMAN AND CEYX:
which returned their bizarre passion
and tried to rise up and embrace the air.

NARRATOR:
The men have lost their belief in their captain, their courage,
their nautical skill, and even their will to live as they wait for the
   end. One weeps
and groans aloud. Another, no braver, is silent, dumbstruck.
One calls on the gods for mercy. Another curses his fate.
And one says one word,

CEYX:
Alcyone,

NARRATOR:
again and again,

CEYX:
Alcyone, my treasure, Alcyone.

NARRATOR:
And this is the end of the world.

[APHRODITE *enters above the sky.*]

CEYX:
O gods, hear my modest prayer: that my body may wash ashore at
    her feet
where she may with gentle hands prepare it to be buried.

[CEYX *sinks below the water.*]

NARRATOR:
Nothing left but the slow parade led by Hermes to the Underworld.

[*Music ends. Everyone but* ALCYONE *exits.* ALCYONE *stirs in her sleep
and begins to count, covering her eyes, like a child who counts to a
certain number, hoping that when she reaches it her wish will be
granted.*]

ALCYONE:
One two three four, fifteen sixteen seventeen eighteen, ninety-eight
ninety-nine, one hundred . . .

[*She uncovers her eyes and looks toward the horizon, then covers her
eyes and begins again.* APHRODITE *enters and watches from the sky.
She summons* IRIS *to watch.*]

One two three four, fifteen sixteen seventeen eighteen, ninety-eight
ninety-nine, one hundred.

[*She uncovers her eyes and looks toward the horizon. She then begins
again and continues under the following lines.*]

APHRODITE:
Look at her, Iris, she's moved her vigil down to the shore
and now she's sleeping there.

ALCYONE:
. . . ninety-eight, ninety-nine, one hundred. Ceyx? Come home. I'm
nearer now, I'm sleeping on the shore. It's not so far until you see me.

[*She begins to count again, quietly.*]

APHRODITE:
This can't go on forever. Go to the house of Sleep and ask him to
arrange a nighttime visitation, a dream that might show our Alcyone
the sorry truth.

[IRIS *departs.* ALCYONE *falls asleep in the shallow waters of the pool.
A* SECOND NARRATOR *appears. As he speaks,* SLEEP *enters, wrapped in
a black velvet blanket, with eyeshades.* APHRODITE *slowly drops white
letter Z's from the sky.*]

SECOND NARRATOR:
Far off in remotest Campania, beyond where the Cimmerians live
in their gloomy caves, is a deeper and even darker grotto,
the home of Sleep. In this place the sun never can, even at midday,
penetrate with the faintest beams. In that cloudy twilight
no rooster dares disturb the silence with his rude crowing,
no dog or nervous goose gives voice to challenge the passing
stranger. Not even branches sigh in occasional passing breezes,
but an almost total silence fills the air.

[SLEEP *snores.* IRIS *creeps in, wearing an illuminated rainbow-colored
skirt and carrying an alarm clock.*]

At the heart of an almost painted stillness,
in a huge, darkened chamber, the god himself relaxes,
drifting in languor. Around him the fragments of ill-assorted
dreams hover over the floor in grand profusion like leaves
the trees have let go to float through the currents of air and fall
in their gorgeous billows below.

IRIS:
Hello?

SECOND NARRATOR:
Into this strange and breathless place, Iris the rainbow intrudes.

IRIS:
O Somnolent One? Somnolent One? Wake up!

SLEEP:
Wha—?

IRIS:
Mildest of all the gods, soother of souls, and healer of wearied
and pain-wracked bodies and minds—

SLEEP:
Iris! Let me rest a moment.

[*He sleeps a bit. Wakes up.*]

Iris! What do you want?

IRIS:
Devise, if you can, some form to resemble King Ceyx

and send it down in a dream to his wife, the Queen Alcyone.
Let her know the news of the wreck of his ship and the death
of the husband she loves so well. Sleep [*she yawns*] do this for us—
can you?

[*She yawns and falls asleep with him for a moment, but luckily her
alarm goes off, startling them both. She runs away.*]

Farewell!

SLEEP [*calling*]:
Morpheus! Mor-phe-us! Come and change your shape
to that of King Ceyx. Go to his wife and tell her [*yawning*]
. . . tell her he is dead.

[MORPHEUS *enters as* CEYX. SLEEP *sees him.*]

That's good. That's very good. Now go!

[SLEEP *stumbles away.* CEYX, *shrouded, approaches* ALCYONE. *She stirs.*]

ALCYONE:
Sir, you seem like a seafaring man, can you tell me,
Where is my husband, Ceyx? Have you seen him on the sea?
When is he coming home? His ship is strong and unmistakable.
Have you seen him? [*Pause.*] Sir?

CEYX [*dropping his shroud*]:
Do you not know me? Has death undone me so?

ALCYONE:
No!

CEYX:
Look at me, I charge you—look at me.

ALCYONE:
No! I won't. I won't!

CEYX:
Look at me, and know your husband's ghost.
Your prayers have done no good,
for I am gone, beyond all help or hope forever.

ALCYONE:
Go away!

CEYX:
I am not some bearer of tales, but the man himself
to whom it happened. Look at me, my little bird.

ALCYONE:
I told you. I knew it would happen and I begged you
not to go. I knew the day you sailed I had lost you forever.
The ship, my hopes, and my life grew smaller
all at the same time. You should have allowed me to come—

CEYX:
Little bird—

ALCYONE:
This is no good, no good—that I should be living
and you be elsewhere or nowhere? I'm drowning now
in the air, I'm wrecked here on the land
where the currents are just as cold and cruel.

CEYX:
Get up from your bed and put on your mourning clothes.

[*He begins to go.*]

ALCYONE:
Wait for me! Come back! Where are you going?
Wait and I'll go with you
as wives are supposed to go with their husbands.

[*But he is gone.*]

[*Calling*] Lucina! Lucina! Give me your lantern.

[LUCINA *enters and gives her lantern to* ALCYONE, *who searches the pool with it, stumbling and frantic.*]

Ceyx! Come back! Where are you?
Come back! He was here. Where is he? Where is he?

LUCINA:
All that night she searched along the shore for her drowned,
dreamed husband. But she found nothing, not even footprints,
only wave after wave of black water. When morning came

[*Music begins.*]

she narrowed her eyes to the horizon, and remembered
how she had looked on that other day.

[HERMES *enters carrying* CEYX *and places him in the water.*]

                              She remembered
his last kiss, the way he turned to the ship, could not bear it,
and turned again to her.

ALCYONE:
What is that out there? Oh, it is a man. Alas, poor sailor, for
your wife and . . .

[*She sees that it is* CEYX. *Music ends.*]

LUCINA:
The gods are not altogether unkind. Some prayers are answered.

ALCYONE:
Ceyx, is this how you return to me?

LUCINA:
She began to run to him; but as she ran, crying, a strange thing
    happened.

[ALCYONE *moves slowly toward* CEYX, *transforming. The sound of waves
and seabirds crying comes up.*]

By the time she reached him, she was a bird.
She tried to kiss him with her bill, and by some trick
of the ocean's heaving, it seemed that his head reached up to hers
in response. You ask, How could he have felt her kiss?

APHRODITE:
But better ask, How could the gods not have felt it?
Seen this, and not had compassion?

LUCINA:
For the dead body was changing, restored to life,
and renewed as another seabird.
Together they still fly, just over the water's surface,
and mate and rear their young, and for seven days each winter
Alcyone broods on her nest that floats on the gentled water—
for Aeolus, her father, then keeps the winds short reined
and every year gives seven days of calm upon the ocean—
the days we call the halcyon days.

ERYSICHTHON

[*Music. Transition. Singers come out, and, as they mop or dry the deck, they sing the following song.*]

> Would, oh would, I were a kingfisher
> That flies with the halcyons
> Along the breaking waves, with a fearless heart,
> That noble bird, that holy bird,
> The deep blue of the ocean.

[*A new* NARRATOR *arrives.*]

NARRATOR:
When you see a miracle like that, how can you deny the existence of the gods? Believe it or not, there are some that do. There was a man called Erysichthon, who scorned the gods and declined to sacrifice on their altars or do them honor. Nothing was sacred to him—he only looked for the usefulness of things. One day he found himself in a grove sacred to Ceres.

ERYSICHTHON:
Cut it down.

NARRATOR:
Sir, that tree is centuries old—

ERYSICHTHON:
We need the wood, cut it down.

NARRATOR:
Sir, this is a sacred grove; and this tree is beloved by Ceres.

[CERES *enters above the sky and watches.*]

ERYSICHTHON:
It's only a tree that the goddess likes, but say it was the goddess herself, I'd cut it down just the same.

NARRATOR:
Sir, please—

ERYSICHTHON [*shoving him away*]:
Get off me, you pious son of a bitch!

NARRATOR:
And he tore the tree down.

[*Enormous sound of the tree falling.*]

SPIRIT OF THE TREE [*offstage*]:
Sir.

ERYSICHTHON:
Who's that?

SPIRIT OF THE TREE:
I am the tree itself speaking. My pangs of death are eased by one thing.

ERYSICHTHON:
And what might that be?

SPIRIT OF THE TREE:
That you will never get away with this.

ERYSICHTHON:
Oh, now I'm really frightened.

[*He laughs and goes home to sleep.*]

NARRATOR:
But the goddess Ceres heard the cry of her tree, and her mind immediately began to move upon torments that she might inflict.

CERES:
Oread!

OREAD [*a handmaid, entering*]:
Yes?

CERES:
There is a place in far-off Scythia. Nothing grows there, no wheat, no grass, no trees. There you will find, huddling together, Cold, Fear, and gaunt Hunger. Tell Hunger I command her to visit this brute and establish a home for herself in his belly. I give him to her as a toy.

OREAD:
I will.

CERES:
I would go myself, but it is forbidden for Hunger and me ever to meet.

[OREAD *exits.*]

NARRATOR:
Oread flew off to the Caucasus, a bleak and nightmarish region. There, in a field of stones, crouched Hunger,

[HUNGER *crawls up onto the deck.*]

pulling from between the rocks, with her teeth and filthy fingernails, some tiny bits of moss. Her hair hung down in lank and matted locks. Her eyes were sunken and circled, her lips were slack and cracked. The vaults of her ribs stuck out, as did every bone in her body. One could count the knobs of her spine.

OREAD [*entering*]:
Hunger?

[HUNGER *turns to face her, and* OREAD *is struck with sudden, terrible hunger pains.*]

OREAD:
Ceres commands—or rather permits you—

HUNGER:
Yes?

OREAD [*backing up, starving, as* HUNGER *crawls toward her*]:
To go to—

HUNGER:
Yes?

OREAD:
To go to Erysichthon and . . . and never to leave him until he is finished.

[*Runs off.*]

HUNGER:
Gladly.

NARRATOR:
Hunger crawled through the air to the house of the victim. As she flew overhead, fields withered and men starved. The birds scattered from her path, too weak to fly. It is night when she arrives at Erysichthon's home and curdles through the halls until she finds him sleeping in his room. She wraps cadaverous arms around him in an embrace as strong as love, but quite the opposite of love. She breathes her spirit into his spirit. And he begins to dream.

ERYSICHTHON [*with* HUNGER *clinging to his back*]:
Pastries, cheese, grapes . . .

NARRATOR:
He wakes.

ERYSICHTHON:
Bring me something to eat! Anything! I'm starving!

[ERYSICHTHON *dashes into the pool, attempting to consume it.* HUNGER *clings to his back.*]

NARRATOR:
But he can't wait to be served. He begins to eat everything in sight: meal after meal after meal after meal. But he can't shake this hunger.

ERYSICHTHON:
More! I need more! More to eat!

NARRATOR:
Baked shrimp and marshmallows, salami and ice cream, liver and doughnuts, everything in every possible combination. Even as he eats he is planning other menus and complaining of his hunger. As the ocean ingests the water from the rivers of the world but still is never filled and remains thirsty and guzzles more and more forever, so he calls out for more.

ERYSICHTHON:
It isn't enough. It isn't enough!

NARRATOR:
His gorging empties the larder and storerooms, the warehouses and barns of the city. His hunger is unabated. What is left to sell?

ERYSICHTHON:
Mother?

MOTHER [*entering*]:
My son?

ERYSICHTHON:
Come with me.

[ERYSICHTHON'S MOTHER, *delighted, goes to fetch her purse and hat.
The* BUYER *enters with an oar, eating an apple.*]

NARRATOR:
Now this part is true, though you may not believe it: His hunger led
him to sell his poor, his darling mother.

BUYER:
She doesn't look so strong.

ERYSICHTHON:
She is, she is. We've had her forever.

BUYER:
I can't give you much . . .

ERYSICHTHON:
Just give—just whatever—just give it to me—

BUYER:
All right then.

[*Tosses him a coin.*]

NARRATOR:
With the few coins he received, he ran home to eat. Riding in a boat
behind her new master, Erysichthon's mother leaned over the hull
and prayed to someone she once knew.

MOTHER:
Poseidon, if you remember me, come and save me now.

[POSEIDON *swims toward* ERYSICHTHON'S MOTHER.]

NARRATOR:
From the briny deep, Poseidon heard her prayer, pulled her into the water, and changed her back into the little girl who used to play along his shores. The salty water licked the years away, until she emerged: the one who gave him praise in childhood, shouting as she ran among the waves. This is the kind of sweet, unbidden praise the gods adore and do not forget.

[*The* BUYER *notices the* MOTHER *is gone and sees the little girl on shore.*]

BUYER:
Hey! Hey you, little girl! Listen up! Where is the old woman who was here a moment ago? Did she dive overboard and swim up to shore?

MOTHER [*now a child*]:
Sir, I swear by the god of the sea that no one except myself has come to this shore. I swear it!

NARRATOR:
To this day, at every hour, somewhere in the world, you can still catch a glimpse of that child playing by the shore.

[*The* MOTHER *exits with* POSEIDON, *and the* BUYER *leaves as well.*]

But let us return to our king. It was not enough. The money she earned for him was not enough for his needs. The emptiness within him was unappeasable. You've seen such men yourself, I'm sure.

ERYSICHTHON:
I need more! I must have more!

NARRATOR:
The godless are always hungry.

ERYSICHTHON:
MORE!

NARRATOR:
Always yelling at waitresses.

ERYSICHTHON:
I WANT MORE!

NARRATOR:
There can be only one end to such a man.

[CERES *comes toward* ERYSICHTHON *with a silver tray holding a plate, a large fork and knife, and a rosebud in a vase. She sets it down on the deck.*]

NARRATOR:
He will destroy himself.

[ERYSICHTHON *goes to the tray, takes off his shoe, places his own foot on the plate, and raises the knife and fork.*]

CERES:
Bon appétit.

ORPHEUS AND EURYDICE

[*Music. Transition. We may see glimpses of various myths:* PANDORA *and her box,* ATALANTA *and the golden apple.*]

NARRATOR:

You've heard of Orpheus, the greatest musician of all time, and his bride Eurydice? His was the unluckiest of wedding days.

[*The sound of wedding bells. The chandelier is fully illuminated.* OR-PHEUS *and* EURYDICE *move toward each other with* ATTENDANTS. *But, as she approaches,* EURYDICE *steps on a snake. We hear a loud hissing, and the joyful wedding bells become funereal. The scene changes to one of mourning, as the dead* EURYDICE *is carried away by* HERMES. *A new* NARRATOR *enters with a music stand and steps into the pool.*]

NARRATOR ONE:

Orpheus and Eurydice: Number One: Ovid, A.D. 8.

[*As he speaks, the Underworld materializes around him. We see* PER-SEPHONE *and* HADES; THE FATES, *snipping their threads;* A SISYPHEAN CHARACTER; *and various other* DENIZENS *of the Underworld.*]

Orpheus, the widower bridegroom, mourned her
in the upper world but his grief was limitless.
Inconsolable, desperate, he left the warmth
and sweetness of our air, he dared to descend
to the River Styx and crossed it to the Underworld.

[*Music begins.*]

Through that dim domain, with all
its shimmering, buried ghosts, he passed,
until he arrived at its melancholy heart
and found its king, lying with Persephone.
He knelt before them, drowning in his grief.

[ORPHEUS *kneels in a shower of water pouring down from above.*]

ORPHEUS:
I don't know what power love has down here,
but I have heard that he has some, for he brought you two together.
If that is true—that passion moved you once—then listen to me:
I've tried to master this grief and I can't.
I understand we all come here in the end.
My bride Eurydice will soon enough be your citizen
in the ripeness of her years. I am asking for a loan,
not a gift. If you deny me, one thing is certain:
I want you to keep me here as well.

[*The shower of water and the music end.*]

NARRATOR ONE:
As Orpheus spoke, the pale phantoms began to weep. Tantalus was no longer thirsty, and Sisyphus sat on his rock to listen.

HADES:
Orpheus, turn around. [*Calling*] Eurydice.

[EURYDICE *enters.*]

Your song has moved us, Orpheus, and you may have her on one condition. As you ascend and leave this place, she will not walk beside you; but she will be following. You must not, until you pass our gates, turn around to look at her. If you look at her before you reach the sunlight, she is ours. Forever.

ORPHEUS:
I understand.

HADES:

Hermes will accompany you. Remember, hesitation or doubt and our gift must be returned. A simple enough condition?

NARRATOR ONE:

It ought to have been. The singer led the way,
ascending the sloping path through the murk.

[ORPHEUS *walks on the deck, followed at a little distance by* EURYD-ICE, *who is limping from the snake bite.* HERMES *follows her.*]

A long way they traveled, almost all the way.
But you know what happened: Concerned for her,
or not quite believing that it wasn't a cruel delusion,
a dream, or a mirage, he turned.

[ORPHEUS *turns around; as he does,* HERMES *lifts* EURYDICE *and pulls her away as she and* ORPHEUS *reach for each other.*]

EURYDICE:

Farewell.

NARRATOR ONE:

That was his last sight of her. But he saw it again and again.

[ORPHEUS, EURYDICE, *and* HERMES *reassemble in their original positions. They walk forward,* ORPHEUS *turns around; as he does,* HER-MES *lifts* EURYDICE *and pulls her away as she and* ORPHEUS *reach for each other.*]

EURYDICE:

Farewell.

NARRATOR ONE:
Is this story a story of love and how it always goes away?

[ORPHEUS, EURYDICE, *and* HERMES *continue to repeat their action. Each time,* EURYDICE *is a little closer to* ORPHEUS *when he turns.*]

EURYDICE:
Farewell.

NARRATOR ONE:
Is this a story of how time can move only in one direction?

[*The action repeats.*]

EURYDICE:
Farewell.

[*The action repeats.*]

NARRATOR ONE:
Is this story a story of an artist, and the loss that comes from sudden self-consciousness or impatience?

[*The action repeats.*]

EURYDICE:
Farewell.

[NARRATOR ONE *exits as* NARRATOR TWO *enters and places her music stand in the water. During the following,* ORPHEUS, EURYDICE, *and* HERMES *walk slowly and continually around the periphery of the pool.*]

NARRATOR TWO:

Orpheus and Eurydice: Number Two. Rainer Maria Rilke. A.D. 1908.

ORPHEUS:

He said to himself, they had to be behind him;
said it aloud and heard it fade away.
They had to be behind him, but their steps
were ominously soft. If only he could
turn around, just once.

NARRATOR TWO:

But looking back would ruin this entire work, so near
completion.

ORPHEUS:

Then he could not fail to see them,
those other two, who followed him so softly:

HERMES:

The god of speed and distant messages,
a golden crown above his shining eyes,
his slender staff held out in front of him,
and little wings fluttering at his ankles;
and on his left arm, barely touching it: *she*.

NARRATOR TWO:

A woman so loved that from one lyre there came
more lament than from all lamenting women;
that a whole world of lament arose, in which
all nature reappeared: forest and valley,
road and village, field and stream and animal;
and that around this lament-world, even as

around the other earth, a sun revolved
and a silent star-filled heaven, a lament-
heaven, with its own disfigured stars—:
So greatly was she loved.

EURYDICE:
But now she walked behind the graceful god,
her steps constricted by the trailing graveclothes,

NARRATOR TWO:
uncertain, gentle, and without impatience.

EURYDICE:
She was deep within herself, like a woman heavy
with child, and did not see the man in front
or the path ascending steeply into life.
Deep within herself. Being dead
filled her beyond fulfillment. Like a fruit
suffused with its own mystery and sweetness,
she was filled with her vast death, which was so new,
she could not understand that it had happened.

HERMES:
She had come into a new virginity
and was untouchable; her sex had closed
like a young flower at nightfall, and her hands
had grown so unused to things that the god's
infinitely gentle touch of guidance
hurt her, like an undesired kiss.

NARRATOR TWO:
She was no longer that woman with brown eyes

who once had echoed through the poet's songs,
no longer the wide couch's scent and island,
and that man's property no longer.

EURYDICE:
She was already loosened like long hair,
poured out like fallen rain,
shared like a limitless supply.

[ORPHEUS *slowly turns to look at her.*]

NARRATOR TWO:
And when, abruptly,
the god put out his hand to stop her, saying,
with sorrow in his voice:

HERMES:
He has turned around—

NARRATOR TWO:
she could not understand, and softly answered,

EURYDICE:
Who?

[*She looks at* HERMES, *who then looks at* ORPHEUS. *Then she looks at*
ORPHEUS.]

Far away,
dark before the shining exit-gates,
someone or other stood, whose features were
unrecognizable.

[*She looks back to* HERMES, *and then slowly turns and walks away, back to the Underworld.*]

ORPHEUS:
He stood and saw how, on the strip of road among the meadows,
with a mournful look, the god of messages
silently turned to follow the small figure
already walking back along the path,
her steps constricted by the trailing graveclothes,

NARRATOR TWO:
uncertain, gentle, and without impatience.

POMONA AND VERTUMNUS
(WITH NARCISSUS INTERLUDE)

[*Music. Everyone leaves the stage. In the silence that follows, two performers enter. One begins to mop the deck; the other (*NARCISSUS*) moves to strike the music stand from the water. But as he starts to exit, he catches sight of his reflection in the pool. It arrests him. He leans down to it. He becomes still. The other performer finishes mopping and notices the stillness of her companion. She tries to move him, but he is paralyzed. She looks offstage impatiently. A third performer enters, carrying a potted narcissus. He hands the plant to the first performer. In one motion, he lifts the second performer, and the first performer fills the newly empty position with the plant. Everyone leaves, the third performer carrying the second, still-frozen performer. A new* NARRATOR *enters.*]

NARRATOR:
There lived at one time a wood nymph named Pomona

[POMONA *enters, skipping and swinging a basket of flowers. She skips around the periphery of the pool throughout the following.*]

whose skill in the care of plants and trees has never been equaled. She hardly noticed the rivers and forests but loved the fields and orchards. These were her passion, her life. She didn't disdain Aphrodite as much as ignore her. She kept aloof from any suitor.

[VERTUMNUS *enters with his suitcase full of his disguises.*]

There was however, one suitor, the god of springtime, Vertumnus. He was

VERTUMNUS:
in love

NARRATOR:
with her—more than all the rest.

VERTUMNUS:
He adored her.

[*Throughout the following,* VERTUMNUS *quickly takes on his various disguises, to little or no effect on the skipping* POMONA.]

NARRATOR:
In the manner of the shyer gods he used to disguise himself, would put on the clothes of a farmhand, wear a straw hat and a working man's shirt, and stick hay stalks behind his ears, to look like some storybook yokel.

VERTUMNUS:
Howdy!

NARRATOR:

When that produced nothing, he thought he might hold in his hand a pruner, trying to look like a field hand who tends the grapes in their arbors. After the complete failure of that, he came with a ladder, to seem as though he were bound for some nearby orchard to gather apples. With wigs, costume, and makeup, he once tricked himself out as a soldier, romantically returned from foreign wars. Another time, he set himself up as an ordinary fisherman fishing in her path on the chance she might pass by. He waited from dawn to dusk, passing from boredom to terror and back again.

VERTUMNUS:

The point was just to be near her,

NARRATOR:

stand there and gaze at her beauty,

VERTUMNUS:

and maybe to wish her good morning

NARRATOR:

or

VERTUMNUS:

good afternoon

NARRATOR:

or

VERTUMNUS:

good evening

NARRATOR:
before he plodded on by.

VERTUMNUS:
I live for these trivial moments!

NARRATOR:
One day he put on an old woman's dress and a wig and wandered through the green, green hills until he saw his beloved standing in the lavender.

[VERTUMNUS *walks along with a cane, as an old woman, admiring the orchard. He approaches* POMONA, *who has finally stopped skipping.*]

VERTUMNUS:
Lovely, truly lovely. But you, miss, are lovelier still.

[*He dares to kiss her on the cheek, then points out vine and tree.*]

Just look at that, would you? And think how that tree and vine complement each other, complete each other. Separate they aren't much, but together, they're splendid. There's a lesson in that, my dear, one that you might consider. The way you've been keeping to yourself is no good, it's a sad violation of nature, as well as a waste. A lover is what you need to make you complete as a woman. You'd have many choices, I think. As many as Helen. But there is one in particular I'd recommend: Vertumnus. I know him as well as I know myself, and I warrant, I guarantee, that his eyes are for you alone. Consider that he's young, attractive, healthy, and strong. Your tastes, too, are the same, for he likes trees and gardens almost as much as you. Besides, he's fun and takes on various disguises—it's a game he likes to play. Believe me, you may take these words that I speak as if they were coming from his own mouth.

NARRATOR:
None of this was working.

VERTUMNUS:
Listen, aren't you afraid of offending Aphrodite? Don't you know the story?

POMONA:
What story?

VERTUMNUS:
The story of Cinyras, his daughter Myrrha, and Aphrodite?

[*The characters enter as they are named.* MYRRHA *carries a bunch of red flowers and a fan that is red on one side, white on the other.* APHRODITE *is smoking a cigarette.*]

POMONA:
No.

NARRATOR:
And he began to tell her.

MYRRHA

VERTUMNUS:
Part One: The Mistake.

There was a girl like you named Myrrha, and she too ignored Aphrodite. She wouldn't fall in love. There were suitors everywhere, but she was blind to them. Finally, Aphrodite had had enough, and seized her with a passion.

[APHRODITE *literally seizes* MYRRHA; *the flowers fall into the pool and scatter.*]

POMONA:
So?

VERTUMNUS:
It was a passion for her father.

POMONA:
That isn't true.

VERTUMNUS:
It is.

APHRODITE [*in* MYRRHA's *ear*]:
You can shut yourself in a room, bolt the door,
but love will come through the window.
Draw the curtains, lock the casement,
but love will seep through the walls.
Never think, never think that you can be safe from love.

NARRATOR:
She struggled hard against her passion.

MYRRHA:
O gods, I pray you, keep off this wickedness,
make me a daughter to my parents.
Even to think what I am thinking is a crime—
or is it a crime? Who would condemn
such love as crime? The animals, I've seen,
will do as they desire. A ram goes to the ewe
that he has sired; and birds will make a nest

with those the nest once held. How happy
they are to be so free!
                    But we have laws.
Yet there are countries, I have heard,
with no such laws, where in the dark,
the bonds of love, already strong, might
be made perfect.
                    Why do I keep thinking
of such things? Leave me alone! He is the best of men—
the best of *fathers*. If I were not his daughter
then I might lie with Cinyras—
but I am his daughter. You have been
virtuous in body, Myrrha; now be so in mind.

[*She struggles free of* APHRODITE *and crouches in a corner of the pool.*]

CINYRAS:
Myrrha?

MYRRHA:
Father?

CINYRAS:
Why are you crying?

MYRRHA:
It's nothing. Nothing.

CINYRAS:
Why should a girl like you be sad? There are suitors at our door every day, yet you keep refusing them, and weeping in the corners of the house. Is there someone special you are hiding?

MYRRHA:
No.

CINYRAS:
What are you waiting for?

MYRRHA:
Nothing.

CINYRAS:
None of them pleases you?

MYRRHA:
No.

CINYRAS:
What sort of husband would you like?

MYRRHA:
One like you.

CINYRAS:
May you always be such a good, sweet girl.

APHRODITE [to *the audience while* MYRRHA, *in her dreams, encounters her father*]:
Midnight came, and sleep crept in the palace
to fold men in his arms. But Myrrha could not sleep.
Tangled in a dream of her father she tossed
all night long, caught between her shame and her desire;
like a tree once wounded by the woodman's ax,
that leans first one way in the wind, then another,
hesitates, but always falls.

VERTUMNUS:
Part Two: The Solution.

[*A noose appears.* MYRRHA *starts to move toward it. Her* NURSEMAID *enters and sees.*]

NURSEMAID:
Myrrha, what are you doing? My child, what are you doing?

MYRRHA:
Nurse, leave me alone!

NURSEMAID:
What is it? I'll help you, whatever it is. The old are not altogether
    helpless.
Has someone bewitched you? Spells may be broken.
Or have you crossed some god? Still you may look to appease
by sacrifices and prayers even the heavens' anger.
What else can it be? Your mother and father are well—

[MYRRHA *sighs.*]

I know. It is love. It must be love. But I can help you.
Whatever it is, whatever you want, I swear by the gods to help you.
Only tell me. Your father will never know—

MYRRHA:
Go away!

NURSEMAID:
But why—?

MYRRHA:
Go away or stop it! Stop asking why I grieve.
It's a crime, the thing you're trying to learn, a crime!

VERTUMNUS:
This went on and on. But the old nurse would not give up.

MYRRHA:
O Mother, Mother, happy in your husband!

NURSEMAID:
What does your mother have to do wi—? Oh, child. Whisper in my
    ear, and tell me I am wrong.
[MYRRHA *whispers.*] I swore to help you and now I must. [*They em-
    brace.*]
Tomorrow your mother leaves for the Feast of Ceres. She'll be gone
    nine days.
Your father will drink. He will be likely—as any man can be—to
    listen to my suggestion

[*The scene slides away from* MYRRHA *and toward* CINYRAS *without
break.*]

that a pretty girl adores you, loves you, and wants to visit
your bedroom. Can she?

CINYRAS:
She's attractive?

NURSEMAID:
Yes, and young.

CINYRAS:
How young?

NURSEMAID:
Your daughter's age.

CINYRAS:
All right then.

NURSEMAID:
There's only one condition. She's very shy and is afraid
for you to see her.

CINYRAS:
How charming.

[*The* NURSEMAID *removes her headscarf and blindfolds* CINYRAS.]

VERTUMNUS:
Part Three: The Corridor.

APHRODITE:
In the small hours of the night, when all was still in the palace, when
the moon had fled from the sky and the stars were concealing themselves in a shroud of cloud, she set out for her father's apartment. She
stumbled, recognized this as an omen, but nevertheless turned down
the hallway.

[*An owl screeches.*]

She continued down the corridor, clutching her nurse's arm for sup-
port. The hall is apparently endless, but then—too soon—they arrive
at the door.

NURSEMAID:
Your girl is here.

VERTUMNUS:
Part Four: Unnameable.

[CINYRAS *wades slowly toward* MYRRHA. *He touches her, lifts her. They lie down, kiss, and are submerged in the water.* MYRRHA *pulls away and leaves him.*]

APHRODITE:
Full of her father, the girl slips out of the room; guilty but shameless.

MYRRHA:
There's nothing to fear or to hope for now.

APHRODITE:
The next night, she returns.

MYRRHA:
Because twice is no worse than once.

[*The father and daughter encounter each other again.* MYRRHA *departs.*]

APHRODITE:
And the third night she's back again.

[*They encounter each other again.*]

CINYRAS:
Let me see you.

MYRRHA:
No.

CINYRAS:
I want to see you.

MYRRHA:
No.

CINYRAS:
Let me see you.

MYRRHA:
No!

[*He pulls off his blindfold. He sees her for a long moment. Then, with a cry, he lunges toward her and tries to drown her. Finally, she escapes. He runs off.*]

NURSEMAID:
She escaped into darkness, out of the room, the house, the city, into
    remote
and exotic lands, even as far as the Arab wilderness.

[*Music begins.*]

MYRRHA:
O Gods, I pray you, change me; make me something else; transform
    me entirely;
let me step out of my own heart.

VERTUMNUS:
Someone must have heard her prayer—for she did change.

APHRODITE:
Some say she changed into a tree;

NURSEMAID:
some say she gave birth to a boy called Adonis;

NARRATOR:
others contend that she dissolved into tears.

APHRODITE:
And this last was not a mere expression, some rhetorical turn
or poetic and hyperbolic trope, but simply the unadorned,
terrible truth. She stepped into a shimmering stream and
began to dissolve: Her body melted.

[*Music rises as* MYRRHA *melts into the pool and vanishes. Music ends.*]

VERTUMNUS [*to* POMONA]:
And then she was gone.

NARRATOR:
This story got Vertumnus nowhere.

POMONA [*to* VERTUMNUS]:
Why are you wearing that ridiculous wig?

VERTUMNUS:
I don't know. I thought—

POMONA:
Take it off. [*He does.*] And take off that idiotic dress.

VERTUMNUS:
I'm embarrassed—

POMONA:
Take it off.

NARRATOR:
When at last the god revealed himself just as he was, much to his surprise, he had no need of words. Little Pomona was happy with what she saw, unadorned and undisguised. Soon enough, the vine was clinging to the tree.

PHAETON

[*Music. Transition. The stage is cleared.* PHAETON *enters, wearing sun glasses and carrying a yellow rubber raft. He tests the water with his toe, then launches his raft and goes to lie on it. The* THERAPIST *enters with her notepad and sits in a chair on the deck of the pool. Music ends. Throughout the following,* PHAETON *floats on his yellow raft. He does not exactly hear the* THERAPIST *when she speaks to the audience, or perhaps he just isn't paying attention.*]

THERAPIST:
Go on.

PHAETON:
Well, my parents were separated when I was really little. Before I was even born. It was a sort of a one-night sort of thing—except it was in the day, in a meadow, where my mother went to watch my father pass by every day. Anyway, I always knew who he was, and I would see him pass by every day—of course—who doesn't? But I never knew him, and he wasn't really around. I mean, not *around* around.

THERAPIST:

Where better might we find a more precise illustration of the dangers of premature initiation than in this ancient tale of alternating parental indulgence and neglect?

PHAETON:

I went to an expensive school and there were a lot of boys there who were, you know, sons of the rich and famous. And one day we're all on the playground and this one kid, Epaphus, he goes to me, "So Phaeton blah blah who's your father, what does he do? Blah blah blah." So I tell him my father's the sun and he says, "Tell me another," and I say, "He's the sun, he's Phoebus Apollo." And he just basically trampled me, just basically beat the shit out of me. Like I was lying.

THERAPIST:

Neither his own opinion of himself, nor the regard for him or lack of it in his peers, obviates the father's primitive role as initiating priest for the younger being. Now, it cannot be contested that the absence of this figure is, for the son, an almost irredeemable loss.

PHAETON:

So I go home and I say, Mom this happened, you know at school. And she gets all upset, crying and everything, because she still loves him and it's an insult to her as well. And I'm like, well, if it's true how come there's no proof of it? It's unfair to us, you know, that there's no proof. And she gets more upset and she says: "Hear me, my child. In all his glory, your father looks down upon us. By his splendor, I swear that you are his truly begotten son. That fiery orb you see crossing the sky each day whose heat enlivens and enables the world and orders our days and nights is indeed your sire. Believe me, my darling!" Blah, blah, blah.

THERAPIST:

When he matures beyond the customary Eden of the mother breast, the child seeks to individuate beyond its enfolding gate and turns to the new symbols of the paternal realm, thus beginning his spiritual passage from one sphere to the next.

[*At this point* PHAETON's *father,* APOLLO, *enters upstage, carrying a music stand. Throughout the rest of the scene he sings "Un' Aura Amorosa" from* Cosi Fan Tutti, *in Italian, softly, under the entire text. Occasionally, when* PHAETON *quotes him in his narrative,* APOLLO *echoes his son in English, all the while never departing from the melody of the song but sliding seamlessly between the Italian lyrics and the English text.* PHAETON *pauses only slightly between* APOLLO's *English phrases. He neither sees his father nor acknowledges his presence.*]

PHAETON:

So she tells me to go over to the valley where my dad goes to work every morning and just ask him to set things straight. To, you know, "do right by me." So I set out and it's hot and it's dusty and it's a long way—across Ethiopia. And I hitch part of the time and part of the time I walk and finally, *finally,* I get there. And the hill is steep.

THERAPIST:

But this passage is never easy.

PHAETON:

At the door are my dad's secretaries, the days and the hours and the century, but they recognize me and they say go on in. And there he is all shining and golden, and I can't even look at him he's so bright. And you know what he says to me? He says, "My son, you are welcome."

64

APOLLO [*singing underneath*]:
My son, you are welcome . . .

PHAETON:
"Speak, Phaeton, to your father."

APOLLO:
Speak, Phaeton, to your father.

PHAETON:
I cannot even tell you what this was to me. So I tell him everything, you know, I just spill my guts. He listens to me and he says, "Let me grant you a favor,

APOLLO:
Let me grant you a favor . . .

PHAETON:
whatever you ask shall be yours."

APOLLO:
Whate'er you ask, shall be yours.

PHAETON:
And he swears to it.

THERAPIST:
The conventional exordium of the initiate from latent to realized potential is inevitably accompanied by a radical realignment of his emotional relationship with the imago of parental authority.

PHAETON:
Now, there's only one thing I want, I mean it's obvious, right? I say,

"Give me the keys to your car." *Immediately,* he starts backpedaling, saying it's his job

APOLLO:
 It's my job . . .

PHAETON:
and no one else can do it,

APOLLO:
 You can't do it.

PHAETON:
and that up in the sky there are the bull and the lion and the scorpion

APOLLO:
 There's a scorpion.

PHAETON:
to get me, and I say, "Give me the keys to your car. I want to drive it myself across the sky. It's my turn. You promised. I want to light the world today."

THERAPIST:
The father, or his substitute, must be assured, before he transfers the symbols of adult vocation, that the son no longer is operating from infantile complexes—complexes that might dangerously redirect his new task through the unconscious promptings of self-aggrandizement, personal preference, or even resentment.

PHAETON:
Where have you been all my life, Dad? It's my turn. Hand it over! So

he hands over the reins, but he won't stop giving advice. You know, like "Don't fly too high,

APOLLO:
Don't fly too high . . .

PHAETON:
nor too low, stay in the tracks, go slantwise."

APOLLO:
Go slantwise . . .

PHAETON:
On and on. But I didn't listen.

THERAPIST:
Myths are the earliest forms of science.

PHAETON:
It was over before it began. It was chaos, okay? Out of control, as if no one was driving. You know, my knees were weak, I was blind from all the light. I set the earth on fire. And I fell. And it just destroyed me—you know, I was just completely and utterly destroyed. O-V-E-R. Over.

[APOLLO's *song ends.* PHAETON *rises abruptly and leaves the stage.* APOLLO *exits.*]

THERAPIST:
It has been said that the myth is a public dream, dreams are private myths. Unfortunately we give our mythic side scant attention these days. As a result, a great deal escapes us and we no longer understand

our own actions. So it remains important and salutary to speak not only of the rational and easily understood, but also of enigmatic things: the irrational and the ambiguous. To speak both privately and publicly.

EROS AND PSYCHE

[*Music. Transition. A raft, covered in red fabric, and bound with gold rope, is placed in the water. Q and A enter and sit on diagonally oppo-site corners of the deck. The doors open and* EROS *enters. He is winged, naked, blindfolded, and carrying a golden arrow. Throughout the fol-lowing he will come forward and lie down to sleep on the raft in the water.*]

Q:
Who is this?

A:
This is Eros, god of love.

Q:
Why does he have wings?

A:
So he can move quickly from body to body.

Q:
Why is he naked?

A:
To make us transparent.

Q:
To make us what?

A:
Transparent in our love. Foolish to others. Exposed.

Q:
Why is he blind?

A:
He is always pictured blind, but he really isn't.

Q:
Because in love we are so ignorant and so compulsive?

A:
There's that.

Q:
What else?

A:
He is blind to show how he takes away our ordinary vision, our mistaken vision, that depends on the appearance of things.

[EROS *lies down on the raft to sleep. Throughout the following,* PSY-CHE *enters, carrying a candelabra. She makes her way down the stairs and along the deck, very slowly and quietly.*]

Q:
Who's this coming down the stairs?

A:
Her name is Psyche.

Q:
Psyche? Her name is Psyche?

A:
Yes.

Q:
What's she doing here?

A:
She's married to the god, but she's never seen him.

Q:
Why is that?

A:
He forbids it.

Q:
How did they meet?

A:
Psyche was so beautiful, the goddess Aphrodite hated her. She sent her son to punish her, but he fell in love instead.

Q:
Does she know that he is a god?

A:
No. She suspects he is a monster.

[PSYCHE *is startled by something. She looks over her shoulder, then
continues along the deck.*]

Q:
Have they had sex already?

A:
Oh yes.

Q:
And how was that?

A:
It was good.

Q:
Then why does she suspect he is a monster?

A:
Her jealous sisters told her so.

[PSYCHE *is startled again. Then she continues.*]

Q:
And she listened to them?

A:
Unfortunately, yes.

Q:
So now she's coming to see him as he sleeps?

A:
Yes.

Q:
To make certain.

A:
Yes.

Q:
With her eyes.

A:
Yes. She's very young. It happens all the time.

Q:
She doesn't trust what she has felt herself?

A:
Not with the radical trust we need.

[PSYCHE *steps into the pool. She moves slowly, so as not to make noise. She approaches the sleeping* EROS *and holds the candelabra over him, looking. This happens in silence.*]

Q:
What does the word "Psyche" mean?

A:
In Greek it means "the soul."

[*Wax from the candles falls on* EROS. *He wakes suddenly and turns abruptly toward* PSYCHE. *They stare at each other a long moment. Then, in one motion, she extinguishes the candelabra in the water. She and* EROS *begin to separate under the following.*]

Q:
What's going to happen to her now?

A:
She's going to suffer.

Q:
And?

A:
She's going to suffer.

Q:
And?

A:
She's going to suffer.

Q:
What does she have to do?

A:
She is given horrible and lonely tasks by Aphrodite.

Q:
Such as?

A:

Sorting thousands of little seeds one from the other.

Q:

How did she manage?

A:

Some little insects help her.

Q:

Like in fairy tales?

A:

Like in all the fairy tales.

Q:

What else?

[PSYCHE *sinks into the water.*]

A:

She had to go down to the Underworld, fetch various things.

Q:

Wasn't she afraid?

A:

She was petrified, but she did it all the same.

Q:

Wasn't it hopeless?

A:

It was hopeless, but she did it all the same.

Q:

What did Love do in the meantime?

A:

He healed his little wound. It hurt him so much when she looked at him like that. The wax from the candle fell on him and burnt him.

Q:

How does it end?

A:

She finishes her tasks and Zeus declares enough's enough.

Q:

He overrides Love's mother?

[EROS *and* PSYCHE *look at each other. They begin to move toward each other.*]

A:

Yes. And further, he gives Psyche a special potion and she becomes immortal. Then he declares that their marriage will last forever.

Q:

Does it?

A:

Of course.

Q:
So it has a happy ending?

A:
It has a very happy ending.

[EROS *and* PSYCHE *approach the raft and sit on it together.*]

Q:
Almost none of these stories have completely happy endings.

A:
This is different.

Q:
Why is that?

[PSYCHE *and* EROS *kiss. And kiss again.*]

A:
It's just inevitable. The soul wanders in the dark, until it finds love. And so, wherever our love goes, there we find our soul.

Q:
It always happens?

A:
If we're lucky. And if we let ourselves be blind.

Q:
Instead of watching out?

A:
Instead of always watching out.

[*Silence.*]

PSYCHE [*turning out to the audience*]:
If you will indulge us, we have one more tale to tell: a coda, if you will.

BAUCIS AND PHILEMON

[*Music. Transition. The raft and candelabra are struck.*]

NARRATOR ONE:
It happened that one night, Zeus, the lord of the heavens, and Hermes, his son, came down to earth to see what people were really like. They disguised themselves as two old beggars, stinking and poor, ragged and filthy. They knocked on a thousand doors.

[ZEUS *knocks on the surface of the deck. Both adopt supplicating poses.*]

ZEUS:
Hello, do you have any spare—?

OFFSTAGE VOICE:
Get out of here! Get the hell out of here! I work hard for my money!

NARRATOR ONE:
And a thousand doors were slammed on them.

[*They knock on the deck, and a* WOMAN *opens the door.*]

HERMES:
Hello, we're tired, we live on the street, and we hoped that you might—

WOMAN AT THE DOOR:
I'm sorry, I'm . . . um . . . soooo sorry. Sorry.

[*She slams the door shut.*]

NARRATOR ONE:
At last they came to a little hut on the outskirts of town.

HERMES:
Why bother knocking here? We've knocked on houses of all kinds, the homes of people with plenty to spare. Whoever lives here obviously has nothing.

ZEUS:
Let's give it a try all the same. We've come all this way.

[*He knocks.*]

HERMES:
This is hopeless. Let's just go ho—

BAUCIS [*entering*]:
Poor strangers! Philemon, there are guests at our door!

ZEUS:
Hello. We are strangers to these parts. We've lost our way and—

PHILEMON [*entering*]:
Baucis, why are you standing there! We must bring our guests inside.

ZEUS:
Do you know us?

PHILEMON:
Of course.

HERMES:
You do?

PHILEMON:
Yes—

HERMES:
Then who are we?

PHILEMON:
Why, you are children of God. Come in, come in.

[*At this point, the narrative divides among several members of the company. They enter and exit variously, carrying illuminated candles in wooden bowls, which stand in for all the items they will mention. They hand these bowls to* BAUCIS *and* PHILEMON, *or place them in the water themselves. The scene is active: The entire surface of the water becomes the "table" being set with illuminated candles.*]

NARRATOR TWO:
The two immortals, satisfied that their disguises had not been seen through, entered the house, lowering their heads to fit through the door.

BAUCIS:
No, don't sit on the floor! Sit on chairs, as quality people do.

NARRATOR THREE:
Philemon ran to get another chair.

NARRATOR FOUR:
And Baucis fetched two pieces of cloth to pad them so the strangers might rest easy.

NARRATOR FIVE:
She stirred the coals in the hearth and fanned the fire to cook them a meal.

NARRATOR ONE:
Philemon set out the embroidered cloth that they saved for feast days.

NARRATOR TWO:
Baucis saw that one of the legs of the chair was short and she propped it up with a shard of a pot.

NARRATOR THREE:
Philemon set out a plate of olives, green ones and black, and a saucer of cherry plums.

NARRATOR FOUR:
Then there was cabbage and some roasted eggs . . .

NARRATOR FIVE:
For dessert there were nuts, figs, dates, and plums.

NARRATOR ONE:
And a basket of ripe apples.

NARRATOR TWO:
Remember how apples smell?

[*A pause. Everyone inhales and remembers. Then they continue.*]

NARRATOR ONE:
At last, with a show of modest pride, they brought out a bit of honey-comb for sweetness.

NARRATOR TWO:
Philemon poured wine from a bottle, but as he filled the glasses of the guests, he saw that the bottle remained full.

ALL NARRATORS:
And then they knew.

[NARRATORS *exit.*]

BAUCIS:
Oh, mercy! Mercy!

[*She runs with her husband to kneel in front of the gods.*]

PHILEMON:
You are divine and we've served you such a simple meal. Baucis, go and kill the goose!

ZEUS:
Let it live. We are gods and we thank you. You've done enough, more than your nasty neighbors thought to do.

[*The original* NARRATOR *of the scene enters with three other members of the company, all carrying bowls of candles. As she speaks, they come forward, kneel in the water, and set the bowls floating. There is music under the next line of* NARRATOR ONE.]

NARRATOR ONE:

Suddenly, everything was changing. The poor little house,
their simple cottage, was becoming grander and grander,
a glittering marble-columned temple. The straw and reeds
of the thatched roof metamorphosed into gold, and gates
with elaborate carvings sprang up, as ground gave way
to marble paving stones.

HERMES:

Old man, old woman, ask of us what you will. We shall grant whatever request you make of us.

[BAUCIS *and* PHILEMON *whisper to each other.*]

BAUCIS:

Having spent all our lives together, we ask that you allow us to die at
the same moment.

PHILEMON:

I'd hate to see my wife's grave, or have her weep at mine.

NARRATOR TWO:

The gods granted their wish. Arrived at a very old age together, the
two stood at what had been their modest doorway and now was a
grandiose facade.

ZEUS:

And Baucis noticed her husband was beginning to put forth leaves,
and he saw that she, too, was producing leaves and bark. They were
turning into trees. They stood there, held each other, and called, before the bark closed over their mouths,

PHILEMON AND BAUCIS:

Farewell.

NARRATOR ONE:
Walking down the street at night, when you're all alone, you can still hear, stirring in the intermingled branches of the trees above, the ardent prayer of Baucis and Philemon. They whisper:

ALL:
Let me die the moment my love dies.

NARRATOR ONE:
They whisper:

ALL:
Let me not outlive my own capacity to love.

NARRATOR ONE:
They whisper:

ALL:
Let me die still loving, and so, never die.

[MIDAS *enters, clutching the stiff, gold jump-rope. Each of his steps is accompanied by the ring of little finger cymbals. He stops on the edge of the deck, kneels, and drops the rope in the water. He washes his face. He reaches into the water and retrieves the jump-rope, now restored to its original state. He looks toward the doors, which open to reveal his* DAUGHTER, *also restored to life. They move toward each other in the pool. She tries two times to embrace him, but he starts away, frightened. The third time, she succeeds. They kneel together in the water. The members of the company all blow out the floating candles.*]

A NOTE ON THE CASTING

The parts in *Metamorphoses* may be divided at the discretion of the director. The original divisions, among five women and five men, were as follows:

FIRST WOMAN: Woman by the Water, Alcyone, Ceres, Atalanta, Attendant at the Wedding/Funeral of Eurydice, Persephone, Pomona, Woman at the Door, Narrator Two of "Baucis and Philemon"

SECOND WOMAN: Scientist, Second Laundress, Narrator of "Alcyone and Ceyx," Erysichthon's Mother, Pandora, Attendant at the Wedding/Funeral of Eurydice, a Fate in the Underworld, Nursemaid to Myrrha, Therapist, Narrator Four of "Baucis and Philemon"

THIRD WOMAN: First Laundress, Sailor, Singer, Lucina, Spirit of the Tree, Eurydice, Narrator of "Vertumnus and Pomona," Q, Baucis

FOURTH WOMAN: Midas's Daughter, Iris, Singer, Hunger, Attendant at the Wedding/Funeral of Eurydice, Denizen of the Underworld, First Performer in "Narcissus Interlude," Myrrha, Narrator Three of "Baucis and Philemon"

FIFTH WOMAN: Third Laundress, Aphrodite, Oread, Attendant at the Wedding/Funeral of Eurydice, a Fate in the Underworld, Narrator Two of "Orpheus and Eurydice," Psyche, First Narrator of "Baucis and Philemon"

FIRST MAN: Zeus, Henchman, Sleep, Erysichthon, Narrator One of "Orpheus and Eurydice," Third Performer in "Narcissus Interlude," Cinyras

SECOND MAN: Midas, Sailor, Narrator of "Erysichthon," Beginning Narrator of "Orpheus and Eurydice," Denizen of the Underworld, Offstage Voice

THIRD MAN: Midas's Servant, Ceyx, Morpheus as Ceyx, Orpheus, Apollo, A, Philemon

FOURTH MAN: Silenus, Sailor, Narrator of the Sleep episode in "Alcyone and Ceyx," Singer, Buyer, Attendant at the Wedding/Funeral of Eurydice, Hades, Narcissus, Phaeton, Eros, Narrator Five of "Baucis and Philemon"

FIFTH MAN: Bacchus, Poseidon, Hermes, a Sisyphean Character, Vertumnus

1. Midas (Raymond Fox) and Silenus (Doug Hara)
Mark Taper Forum, *copyright © Craig Schwartz*

2. Alcyone (Louise Lamson)
Second Stage Theatre, *copyright © Joan Marcus*

3. Orpheus (Erik Lochtefeld)
Second Stage Theatre, *copyright © Joan Marcus*

4. Narcissus (Doug Hara)
Second Stage Theatre, *copyright © Joan Marcus*

5. Vertumnus (Adrian Danzig) and Pomona (Louise Lamson)
Berkeley Repertory Theatre, *copyright © Ken Friedman*

6. Aphrodite (Hallie Beaune Jacobson) and Myrrha (Anjali Bhimani)
Seattle Repertory Theatre, *copyright © Chris Bennion*

7. Phaeton (Doug Hara) and three ensemble members
(Anjali Bhimani, Louise Lamson, and Heidi Stillman)
Second Stage Theatre, *copyright © Joan Marcus*

8. Phaeton (Doug Hara) and Apollo (Erik Lochtefeld)
Seattle Repertory Theatre, *copyright © Chris Bennion*

9. Baucis (Heidi Stillman) and Philemon (Erik Lochtefeld)
Second Stage Theatre, *copyright © Joan Marcus*

10. "Let me die the moment my love dies"—ensemble members Felicity Jones and Chris Kipiniak
Second Stage Theatre, *copyright © Joan Marcus*

Mary Zimmerman is a professor of performance studies at Northwestern University. Her credits as an adapter-director include *The Notebooks of Leonardo da Vinci*, *The Odyssey*, *The Arabian Nights*, *Eleven Rooms of Proust*, and *Journey to the West*. She is the recipient of a MacArthur Fellowship, an ensemble member of Chicago's Lookingglass Theatre Company, and a Manilow Resident Director at the Goodman Theatre.